內含 **8** 的無限力量

<u>This book holds the infinite power of eight</u>

To Generate Wealth

齊來致富

By David.J.Nelson

EIGHT
8
This Book Holds the Infinite Power of Eight
David Nelson

5 Star Reviews

"Great 8! Anyone who has any interest in, or connection to, East Asian philosophy will love this book. You'll never look at an 8 the same!"

Leslie Hutchison, Amazon review July 9, 2018

"Charming little book, especially for anyone who has lived in Asia."

Easy-to-read; Entertaining; Informative; Original; Whimsical; Witty

Daniel F. Keller, BookBub, July 2018

"This book is a must read! Mr. Nelson understands and promotes the power of 8. Since reading this, I appreciate the good fortune associated with this number. Thank You!"

J Jacob, Booksamillion, September 4, 2018

I dedicate this book to my son Andre.

送給我摯愛的兒子

"Everything has beauty, but not everyone sees it."

Confucius

萬物皆有動人之處，然非眾人皆能洞悉

--孔子

TO THE READER

Fascinated is the best word to describe how I felt when I watched people interacting with the number eight during my years living in Asia. Eight has such powerful symbolic and monetary value in that region that it sent me on a journey of discovery. I started to find the number eight everywhere in this world. The more I researched and explored, the more facts I found about this phenomenal number. There is actually substantial history behind eight's power. Ranging across cultures, it is amazing how often the number eight appears prominently in religious literature and in scientific observation. Is the omnipresence of eight's power on the planet just a coincidence? I don't think so. The power of eight envelopes the world everywhere. For now, I want to thank you for joining me on this journey. Now that you have already entered the world of eight with me, just settle back, get comfortable, take a deep breath, and enjoy eight's ride!

致讀者：

「神魂顛倒」，乃是我在亞洲小住時所見----處理與
8 字有關的事情之見聞。8 字擁有很大的力量，不輪在
形式上或金錢上的價值，有見及此，我嘗試尋找世界各
地與 8 字有關的事物。
我越發拙，竟發現很多不尋常之事皆與這數字息息相關。

在不同的宗教領域，文化、科學、歷史也和「8」牽上
不解的關係。是一個又個巧合嗎？我認為---整個世界被
「8」字重重包圍。
現在，就請與我一起深呼吸、安心地進入「8」的世界，
享受「8」的旅程吧！

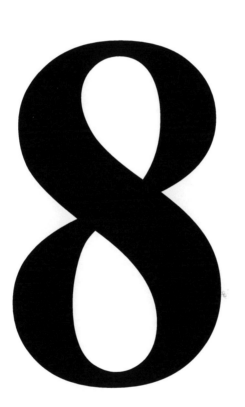

I. Why should you care about the number eight?

1. In Asia, the number eight projects palpable power.

2. Eight holds real value in Asian real estate.

3. People pay more in China for number eight.

4. Number eight Hong Kong license plate sold: $2,300,000.

5. Apartments on the eighth floor are more valuable.

6. Big Chinese success: Beijing Olympics, August eighth, 2008.

7. Not only China, but all Asia values eight.

8. You read eight sentences: now luck you have.

I.　為甚麼「8」如此重要？

1.　「8」在亞洲力量無窮

2.　在房地產佔高價值

3.　中國人願付高價

4.　「8」字車牌達 2 百萬

5.　「8」樓住宅的價值

6.　北京奧運：08 年 8 月 8 日

7.　全亞洲對「8」的重視

8.　此書使你致富

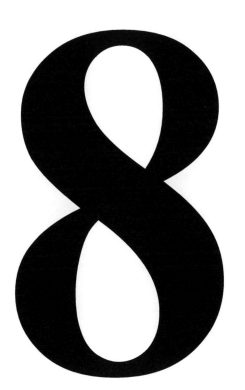

II. Here are some facts about the number eight.

1. Eight in Chinese sounds like "to become rich."

2. The atomic number designation for Oxygen is 8.

3. One byte of computer data is 8 bits.

4. Our solar system still survives with 8 planets.

5. Science says "octonians" have power within string theory.

6. Christians, Buddhists, Hindus, Jewish, and Muslims respect eight.

7. The Jewish celebrate Chanukah for eight days total.

8. Eight is the vertical upright symbol of infinity.

II. 一些與「8」有關的事

1. 中國人：「8」= 發達

2. 氧氣的原子名稱：「8」

3. 電腦 1 Byte = 8 bits

4. 太陽系有 8 大行星

5. 弦理論中含 8 元素

6. 所有宗教都尊重 8

7. 光明節慶祝為期 8 天

8. 把 8 打直=無窮無盡

8

III. The bible is filled with the number eight:

1. Eight is used 73 times in the bible.

2. Jesus Christ was resurrected on the eighth day.

3. The Feast of Tabernacles lasted for eight days.

4. All the Lord's covenants with Abraham totaled eight.

5. There are eight songs in the Old Testament.

6. The number 888 is the symbol of God.

7. Noah's Ark saved a total of eight people.

8. The total number of Elijah's miracles was eight.

III. 聖經與「8」字的關係

1. 聖經用了 73 次「8」

2. 耶穌在第 8 天復活

3. 住棚節歷時 8 天

4. 上帝和亞伯拉罕共立了 8 次約

5. 舊約內有 8 首詩歌

6. 上帝的象徵為：888

7. 挪亞方舟救了 8 人

8. 以利亞行 8 次神蹟

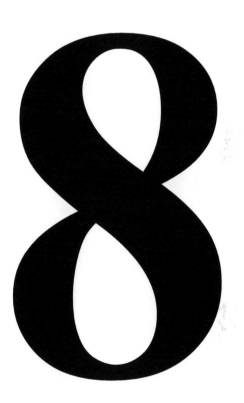

IV. The number eight is also paramount in Buddhism:

1. To achieve Nirvana (enlightenment), the path is eightfold.

2. Understanding, view, thought, speech, effort, action, mindfulness, concentration.

3. Buddhist missionaries brought eight auspicious symbols to China.

4. The circular "Dharmacakra" Buddhist symbol has eight spokes.

5. Buddha emphasized eight attainments also called eight "jhanas."

6. There are eight great Bodhisattvas according to Buddhism.

7. Eight is the exact number of Chinese "Immortals."

8. December eighth is Buddha's Birthday celebration in Japan.

IV. 「8」在佛教的重要性：

1. 通往極樂需達 8 層

2. 明、觀、想、說、行、慎、集(中)

3. 「8」吉祥物帶來中國

4. 佛教旗幟有 8 輪幅

5. 佛教造詣又稱 8 禪

6. 佛教提及有 8 菩薩

7. 佛教中有 8 大眾神

8. 日本佛誕為 12 月 8 日

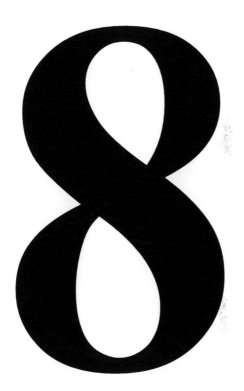

V. Remember and recite a poem about number eight:

1. This poem is about the powerful number eight.

2. Notice the cadence with each sentence of eight.

3. When eight is with me, nothing goes wrong.

4. Eight's energy flows like water, making me strong.

5. Forget what I will, but this I know.

6. My eight enemies flee, my eight allies grow.

7. Eight is more powerful than any single foe.

8. Reap wealth from thoughts of eight I sew.

V. 詩歌與 8 字種種關係

1. 這是一首 8 的誦材，

2. 誦材乃由 8 句組成，

3. 8 字永遠帶我幸運。

4. 強如流水，令我強壯！

5. 即使忘記一切，只知：

6. 敵人逃離，盟友越強

7. 「8」比任何敵人為強

8. 所收割也比想像強。

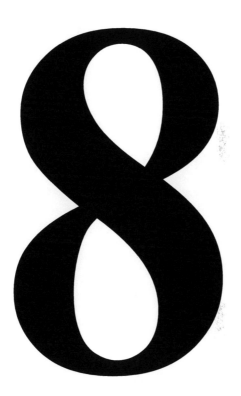

VI. Does scientific evidence point to number eight's power?

1. Science is filled with examples of eight's power.

2. Eight nucleons make complete shells within atomic nucleus.

3. Eight = largest cube number in the Fibonacci sequence.

4. There are exactly eight bits in an Octet.

5. Number of blood types for humans is eight.

6. How many electrons reside in a shell: eight.

7. Eight vertices are needed to form a cube.

8. Light travels from sun to earth: eight minutes.

VI. 「8」與科學種種奧妙

1. 科學充滿 8 的力量

2. 原子核 = 8 核子組成

3. 「8」斐波納契數到最大立方數

4. 八重唱由 8 人合唱

5. 人體血液有 8 種

6. 電子層包含 8 電子

7. 1 立方體有 8 支點

8. 太陽 ⟷ 地球光 1 速：8 分鐘

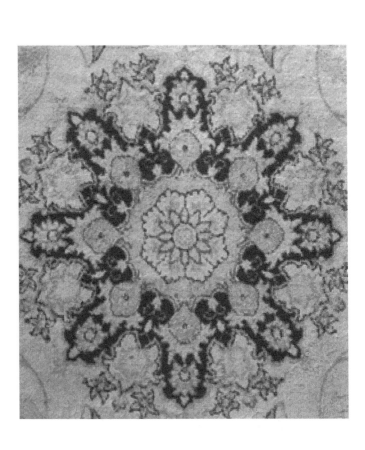

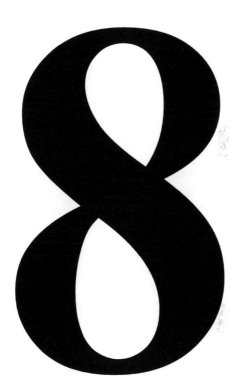

VII. How do you harness the power of eight?

1. You seek out eight in all you do.

2. Imagine eight things that will help you succeed.

3. Attach number eight to all that you own.

4. Always keep eight of something in your pocket.

5. Keep eight dollars, eight Yuan, or eight pesos.

6. Treasure eight of your family who you love.

7. Keep this book with you at all times.

8. Share this book with your eight best friends.

VII. 如何利用 8 的力量？

1. 無論何事也要 8 字

2. 聯想 8 件成功之物

3. 任何事都與 8 聯繫

4. 永遠帶着含 8 的物件

5. 口袋裏永遠有 8 元

6. 重視「8」個至愛親朋

7. 永遠擁有此書：永遠

8. 與 8 好友分享此書

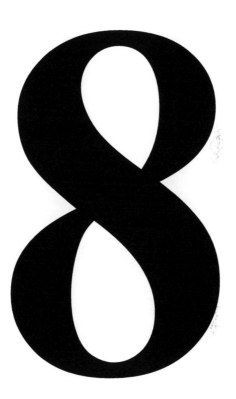

VIII. How the number eight is one with wealth:

1. Old Spanish coins were called "pieces of eight."

2. U.S. Federal reserve note serials have eight digits.

3. The number eight can create wealth for you.

4. Observe significant activity in Asia, August eighth 2018.

5. Plan your business now for the following dates:

6. 2028, 2038, 2048, 2058, 2068, 2078, 2088.

7. Imagine the number eight in your mind now.

8. Hold this book: hold the power of 8.

VIII. 「8」與致富的關係

1. 舊西班牙幣為「8 pieces」

2. 美金編號為 8 位數

3. 「8」能令人 8 來財富

4. 寓意亞洲：8.8.2018 發生的大事

5. 為以下日期安排工作

6. 2028、2038、2048、2058、2068、2078、2088

7. 幻想「8」永在心中

8. 永遠擁有着這本書

Acknowledgements

My son and my wife Letty got me motivated to make the leap from thinking about creating something to actually doing it. Checking me when I was critiquing some art work at the Guggenheim in New York, they told me that it may be true that the artist's work was, perhaps, not that impressive to hold such exorbitant monetary value. However, they said "the difference between this artist and you is that the artist got out there and produced something." Letty looked me in the eyes and said "if you think you could make something better, then you should go and do it."

My dear friend Eric A gave me the idea to structure this work into exactly eight chapters. That ingenious idea brought me to where we ended up today with not only eight chapters but also eight sentences in each chapter- and every sentence contains exactly eight words.

Working in the Philippines introduced me to so many amazing people. One of my colleagues who encouraged me to continue with this project was Paul S. Paul is a genius and a very critical thinker. When he did not shoot the premise of the book down, I knew I was onto something. Thank you for not laughing Paul!

Then there are all the people who have given me love

and support for all or most of my life. Nancy and Jim of course are at the very top of that list. They brought me into this world and then gave me what I needed to survive and to thrive.

Then come my sisters Meg and Danielle. They are two of the strongest and most beautiful women in the world who I love with all my heart. Their father Russ (in memory) was also very influential in my life as he always challenged me to be better.

All of my extended Guandalini family in Connecticut made me into who I am today. Jean, Joe, Judy, Henry, Marian, Dave, Tommy, Pete G, Cindy, Pete H, and all of their families are my heroes and my inspiration.

Letty's mother Rosalina brought the love of my life into this world.

So many wonderful people have surrounded me through this journey of life. All of your names may not be listed here but you know who you are and you know that I love and appreciate you.

鳴謝

吾内子和兒子常鼓勵我實踐夢想,當我仍在美術館(紐約 Guggenheim)從事藝術評論一職時,同事曾告訴我,並不是所有藝術品都有這樣高的價值。

内子也曾鼓勵:「假如你想做一些較有意義的事,不妨一試!」

我的好朋友 Eric 給此書提供不少寶貴意見,他建議我把此書分為 8 個單兀,每單元由 8 句組成,每句則由 8 個未組成。

在菲律賓工作期間,也為我帶來不少好友。其中,同事 Paul.S.鼓勵我繼續完成此書。他是一個天才,也是出色的思考家。他沒有讓我打消寫書的念頭,尤我覺得自己仍可繼續寫下去,這真是一年令人很鼓舞的事。

除此之外,我的四周充滿了愛、我尤其感激我的父母----Nacy 和 Jim 把我帶來這美好的世界,讓我深明生命的意義,以致我能堅強地成長。

Meg 和 Danielle----我的姊妹,她們是全世界最漂亮女性,她們的父親(已故),Russ 也對我有一定的影響,因為他常鼓勵我去接受挑戰。

另外，我的康乃迪克洲(Guandalini) 家族，也成就了今天的我。

多謝Jean、Joe、Judy、Henry、Marian、Dave、Tommy、Peter.G.、Peter.H.及他們所有的家人-----

你們全是我的英雄和靈感的泉源！

About the author

David J. Nelson earned his B.A. in Political Science from the University of Georgia and he also holds a M.A. in International and Comparative Politics from the University of Ottawa. He lives with his wife Letty, his son Andre, and his dog "Julie." The street address of their home is 8.

https://www.facebook.com/Eight-8-2154878644542235/
https://sites.google.com/view/8888eight8888

免責聲明

雖然作者與出版社已努力肯定本書資料無誤，本書作者及出版社均不為此書的疏漏而帶來的損失負上任何責任。

https://www.facebook.com/Eight-8-2154878644542235/
https://sites.google.com/view/8888eight8888

Made in the USA
Coppell, TX
19 October 2019